NEW YORK

LET'S EXPLORE AMERICA

NEW YORK
Valerie Bodden

Published by Creative Education
P.O. Box 227, Mankato, Minnesota 56002
Creative Education is an imprint of The Creative Company
www.thecreativecompany.us

Design and production by Mary Herrmann
Art direction by Rita Marshall
Printed by Corporate Graphics in the United States of America

Photographs by 123RF (Simona Dumitru), Alamy (AGStockUSA, Inc., Content Mine International,
Historical Art Collection, Richard Levine, North Wind Picture Archives, Stock Montage, Inc.), Corbis
(Bettmann, Gaetano, Hulton-Deutsch Collection, The Mariners' Museum, Daniel Mirer, David
Muench), Dreamstime (Elvinstar, Familyfotographer, Gary718, Mako67, Marcusarm, Msavoia,
Onepony), Getty Images (Hulton Archive, Curt Maas, J. Meric, MPI, Gabe Palacio, Harald Sund), and
iStockphoto (Miroslava Arnaudova, Anna Chelnokova, Sebastien Cote, Rusty Dodson, Randy Harris,
Sven Klaschik, William Mahar, Olga Skalkina, Vishwanatha Srinivasan, Denis Jr. Tangney, David Tyrer)

Library of Congress Cataloging-in-Publication Data

Bodden, Valerie.
New York / by Valerie Bodden.
p. cm. – (Let's explore America)
Includes index.
Summary: A basic survey of "The Empire State," exploring its early history, its plant and animal life,
some of its well-known residents, and fun places to visit such as Niagara Falls.
ISBN 978-1-58341-835-2

1. New York (State)—Juvenile literature. I. Title. II. Series.
F119.3.B58 2010
974.7—dc22   2009002723
CPSIA: 040110 PO1139

First Edition
9 8 7 6 5 4 3 2 1

CREATIVE EDUCATION

New York is a state in the northeastern part of America. It is a medium-sized state. New York became a state in 1788. New York is nicknamed "The **Empire** State." This is because it is a powerful state.

TOP, THEN LEFT TO RIGHT:
- New York's Brooklyn Bridge in the late 1800s
- An old map showing New York
- Early American soldiers in New York
- New York soldiers during the Civil War (in the 1860s)
- Big buildings in Albany, New York

The Iroquois *(EER-uh-kwoy)* **American Indians** were some of the first people to live in New York. They were there before it was a state. Henry Hudson was one of the first white people to explore New York. More people moved to New York after that.

TOP, THEN LEFT TO RIGHT:

- *American Indians about 200 years ago*
- *Explorer Henry Hudson and his men meeting Indians*
- *The head of the Statue of Liberty*
- *Immigrants (people moving from one country to another) arriving in New York*
- *A ship carrying immigrants to New York*

Part of New York is next to the Atlantic Ocean. There are beaches there. Other places in New York have hills and **mountains**. New York is usually warm in the summer. But winters can be cold and snowy.

TOP, THEN LEFT TO RIGHT:

• *Heart Lake, in eastern New York*

• *Kids fishing in a New York lake*

• *A motorcycle race on a frozen New York lake in the winter*

• *Hikers climbing in the Adirondack (ad-eh-RON-dak) Mountains*

F armers in New York grow corn, wheat, and apples. Maple and birch trees grow in New York's forests. Deer and foxes live there.

TOP, THEN LEFT TO RIGHT:
- *A New York apple orchard*
- *People collecting sap in a maple tree forest*
- *An old barn on a New York farm*
- *A farmer's corn*
- *A red fox*

New York's state flower is the rose. The rose has soft, colorful petals. New York's state bird is the bluebird. The bluebird has bright blue feathers. New York's state tree is the sugar maple. The sugar maple's **sap** is used to make maple syrup.

TOP, THEN LEFT TO RIGHT:
- *A close-up view of roses*
- *A bluebird*
- *Maple trees with buckets to collect sap*
- *New York roses*

People from all over the world live in New York. Many people in New York work in banks. Some print books. Others make clothes.

Baseball player Lou Gehrig (*GAIR-ig*) was from New York. He was one of the best baseball players ever. Poet Walt Whitman was from New York, too.

- The United Nations building in New York City
- The office for The New York Times newspaper
- New York Yankees baseball players Lou Gehrig (at left) and Babe Ruth (at right)
- A worker making clothes
- A scene from the 1933 movie King Kong, where a giant gorilla climbs New York City's tall Empire State Building

New York City is the biggest city in New York. About eight million people live there. Albany is the capital of New York. The capital is where people in the **government** make decisions about laws for the state.

TOP, THEN LEFT TO RIGHT:

- *Tall buildings called skyscrapers in New York City*
- *Taxicabs (cars that carry people on short trips) in New York City*
- *The state capitol (main government building) in Albany*
- *Grand Central Terminal (train station) in New York City*
- *The New York Supreme Court building in New York City*

E very year, lots of people visit the Statue of Liberty in New York City. Others drive to a huge waterfall called Niagara (*ny-AG-ruh*) Falls. There's always plenty to do in New York!

TOP, THEN LEFT TO RIGHT:
- *Niagara Falls, between New York and Canada*
- *A New York Yankees baseball player*
- *The Statue of Liberty*
- *A Ferris wheel at the Coney Island amusement park*
- *A St. Patrick's Day parade in New York City*

FACTS ABOUT NEW YORK

First year as a state: *1788*

Population: *19,541,453*

Capital: *Albany*

Biggest city: *New York City*

Nickname: *The Empire State*

State bird: *bluebird*

State flower: *rose*

State tree: *sugar maple*

A farm in northern New York

GLOSSARY

American Indians—people who lived in America before white people arrived

empire—a powerful group of lands led by one ruler

government—a group that makes laws for the people of a state or country

mountains—very tall, steep hills made out of rock

sap—a watery substance inside a plant that carries food to different parts of the plant

READ MORE

Burg, Ann E. *E Is for Empire: A New York State Alphabet*. Chelsea, Mich.: Sleeping Bear Press, 2003.

De Capua, Sarah. *New York*. New York: Children's Press, 2002.

LEARN MORE

Enchanted Learning: New York
http://www.enchantedlearning.com/usa/states/newyork/index.shtml
This site has New York facts, maps, and coloring pages.

Kids Konnect: New York
http://www.kidskonnect.com/content/view/196/27
This site lists facts about New York.

A worker in an underground New York salt mine

A sign for a famous New York
City street called Wall Street